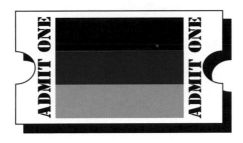

Neuschwanstein
Castle
Built By
King Ludwig II

FACES AND PLACES

GERMANY

BY MARY BERENDES

THE CHILD'S WORLD®, INC.

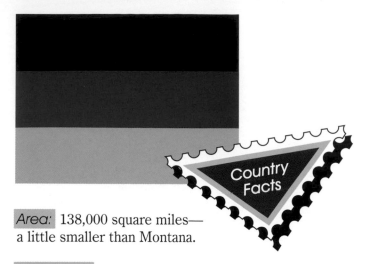

Country Facts

Area: 138,000 square miles—
a little smaller than Montana.

Population: About 82 million people.

Capital City: Berlin.

Other Important Cities: Hamburg, Munich, Cologne, Frankfurt am Main.

Money: The Deutsche (DOYTCH) mark.

National Language: German.

National Song: The third part of a song called "Deutschland–Lied," or
"Song of Germany."

National Holiday: German Unity Day on October 3.

National Flag: Three stripes of black, red, and gold. All three colors stand
for Germany's unity.

Heads of Government: The federal president of Germany and the federal
chancellor of Germany.

Text copyright © 2000 by The Child's World®, Inc.
All rights reserved. No part of this book may be reproduced
or utilized in any form or by any means without written
permission from the publisher.
Printed in the United States of America.

Library of Congress Cataloging-in-Publication Data
Berendes, Mary.
Germany / by Mary Berendes
Series: "Faces and Places".
p. cm.
Includes index.
Summary: Describes the geography, history, people
and customs of Germany.
ISBN 1-56766-598-5 (library : reinforced : alk. paper)

1. Germany — Juvenile literature.
[1. Germany] I. Title.

DD17.B385 1999
943 — dc21
98-43001
CIP
AC

GRAPHIC DESIGN
Robert A. Honey, Seattle

PHOTO RESEARCH
James R. Rothaus / James R. Rothaus & Associates

ELECTRONIC PRE–PRESS PRODUCTION
Robert E. Bonaker / Graphic Design & Consulting Co.

PHOTOGRAPHY
Cover photo: Girl at Oktoberfest Parade
by Adam Woolfit/Corbis

Table of Contents

CHAPTER	PAGE
Where is Germany?	6
The Land	9
Plants and Animals	10
Long Ago	13
Germany Today	14
The People	17
City Life and Country Life	18
Schools and Language	21
Work	22
Food	25
Pastimes	26
Holidays	29
Index & Glossary	32

The world is a beautiful place. From high above, you can see many different colors and shapes on Earth's surface. The deep blue areas are the world's oceans. The white is our swirling clouds. The brown and green patches are land areas called **continents**. Some continents are made up of many different countries. Germany is a country on the continent of Europe.

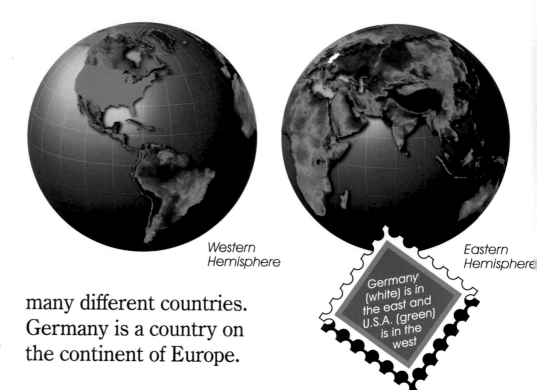

Western Hemisphere

Eastern Hemisphere

Germany (white) is in the east and U.S.A. (green) is in the west

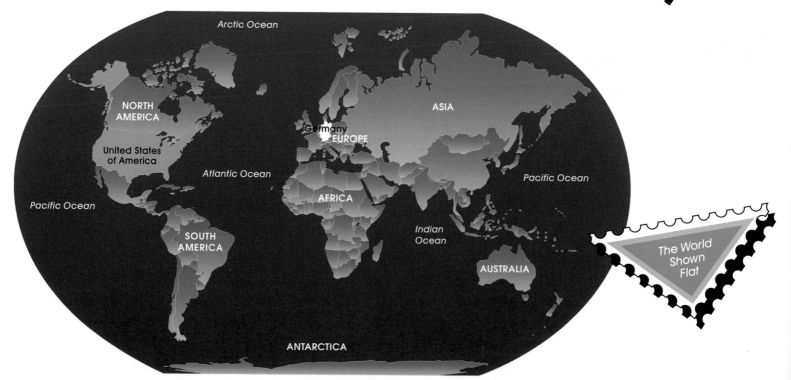

Arctic Ocean

NORTH AMERICA

United States of America

ASIA

Germany EUROPE

Atlantic Ocean

Pacific Ocean

Pacific Ocean

AFRICA

Indian Ocean

SOUTH AMERICA

AUSTRALIA

ANTARCTICA

The World Shown Flat

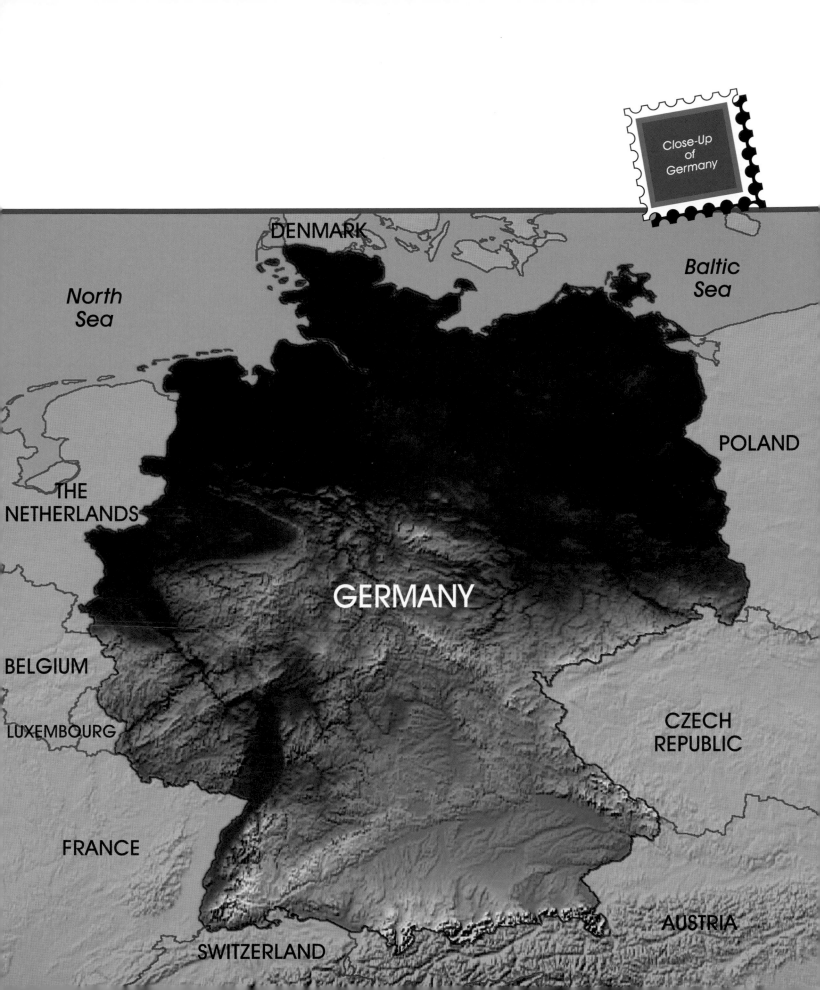

DENMARK

*North
Sea*

*Baltic
Sea*

POLAND

THE
NETHERLANDS

GERMANY

BELGIUM

LUXEMBOURG

CZECH
REPUBLIC

FRANCE

AUSTRIA

SWITZERLAND

Bavarian
Alps
Near
Ramsau

BALTIC
SEA
Rügen Island

Elbe River

BAVARIA

BLACK
FOREST

Titisee   BAVARIAN ALPS   Ramsau
Neuschwanstein

Germany has many types of land. In the north, the land is flat and low. These are Germany's *lowlands*. In the middle of Germany, the land is covered with hills and valleys. In the south, snowy mountains called the *Alps* tower over tiny farms and villages.

Rügen Island In The Baltic Sea

Wolfgang Kaehler/Corbis

Germany also has lots of rivers and forests. The *Black Forest* is famous all over the world. Its trees grow tall and thick—and dark! That's how the forest got its name.

Elbe River Valley From Sandstone Hills

Wolfgang Kaehler/Corbis

Black Forest Near Titisee ("see" means lake)

Wild Country/Corbis

Plants & Animals

Since there are so many kinds of land in Germany, many kinds of plants and trees can be found there. In the deep forests, pine, beech, and oak trees grow. In the fields, colorful wildflowers and grasses live. Many types of bushes and shrubs grow in Germany, too.

Francesc Muntada/Corbis

Animals live in many different areas of Germany. Wolves, deer, grouse, and lynx all make their homes in Germany's forests. Wild pigs and beavers live there, too. Birds of all kinds live everywhere from the flat meadows to the high mountains.

German Red Deer Have Long Antlers

Wild Boar In Schleswig-Holstein

Maurizio Lanini/Corbis

Lynx In Bayerischer Wald Mountains

Uwe Walz/Corbis

SCHLESWIG-HOLSTEIN

•Bonn

Bayerischer Wald
Mountains

Butterfly
And Flowers
Near Bonn

Long Ago Castle Owners Made Shippers Pay To Use The Rhine River

Berlin ☆

Rhine River

Befreiungshalle

People have been living in Germany for more than 100,000 years. The first people were hunters who probably lived in caves. Years later, other groups came to Germany. The many groups often fought over who would rule the country. At one point, the German people united together. Germany became very powerful. It even ruled other countries!

Replica Of The Red Baron's Plane Used In World War I

Over time, Germany lost its power. To become strong again, Germany's leaders built a strong army and navy. Other countries began to worry that Germany would attack them. These countries united together, and soon, World War I began.

Adam Woolfitt/© Corbis

Befreiungshalle (1863) Honors The German People's Struggle Against Napoleon

Government Buildings In Schillerplatz Square, Berlin 1880's

Michael Maslan Historic Photographs/Corbis

13

After a lot of fighting, Germany lost the war. Some of its land was taken away as punishment. Many Germans didn't think this was fair. When Germany tried to gain power again, World War II began. Germany lost again, and was split in half as punishment.

Artist Christo Covered The Reichstag Before Restoration Began, 1995

Manfred Vollmer/Corbis

Today, Germany is whole again. It has a strong government and happy people. Germany no longer tries to fight other countries for power. Instead, its people and government work together for peace.

Robert Maass/Corbis

"We Are One People" Says The Sign In Cottbus, 1990

German Leaders Stood Trial In Nürnberg After World War II

UPI/Corbis-Bettmann

FORMER EAST GERMANY
Berlin ☆ Reichstag
Cottbus •

FORMER WEST GERMANY

Nürnberg •

Berlin Wall Dividing East And West, 1985

Pied Piper
Of Hamlin
Leads
Children
Dressed
As Mice

Rügen Island

Hamlin

Erfurt

BAVARIA

The People

About 82 million people live in Germany. Most are relatives of the different groups that came to Germany long ago. Others are **immigrants**, or newcomers from other countries. Many immigrants come to Germany from Russia and other countries in Europe.

Owen Franken/Corbis

Bavarian Couple Dressed For Local Festival

Germans are kind people who like to smile and laugh. They have a great pride for their country's beautiful forests and mountains, too. Germans also have good imaginations. Many famous fairy tales and stories came from different parts of Germany.

James L. Amos/Corbis

Young People Dancing At Festival In Erfurt

People At A Viewpoint on Rügen Island

Wolfgang Kaehler/Corbis

ADMIT ONE

City Life
And
Country
Life

ADMIT ONE

Obertsdorf
Village
And
Bavarian
Alps

Adam Woolfit/Corbis

Most Germans live in cities or towns. Many people live in apartments. Others live in small houses. German cities are much like those in the United States. There are tall buildings, busy streets, shops, hotels, and restaurants. There are often markets and parks, too.

Farmlands
And Zell On
The Moselle
River

Country life in Germany is quieter. Many families live on small farms raising animals or crops. Others live in tiny towns. Country dwellers are cheerful people. They like to talk and share stories with each other.

Patrick Ward/Corbis

Modern Buildings
In Frankfurt
am Main

Jim McDonald/Corbis

Paul Almasy/Corbis

Rhine
River

Moselle
River
Zell • Frankfurt am Main

Munich

BAVARIAN ALPS
Oberfsdorf

Heidelburg University Building Built In 1700 Is Still In Use

• Dresden

• Heidelburg

• Munich

Children in Germany begin going to school when they are about six years old. They learn writing, reading, math, and science, just as you do. Many children also study music. When they are a little older, some students learn how to speak another language, too.

Gianni Dagli Orti/Corbis

Germany's official language is German. It is from the same group of languages as Norwegian, Swedish, and Dutch. Many German words are also used in the English language. "Kindergarten" is one German word that many people use every day.

Elementary School Student From Dresden

Page From A Teacher's Book That Is 700 Years Old

History Lives In A Greek And Roman Museum In Munich

Owen Franken/Corbis

Adam Woolfitt/Corbis

Work

James L. Amos/Corbis

Germans are very hard workers. In the cities, many people work at banks and big companies. Others work in restaurants, shops, hotels, and factories. Some Germans work on farms or on fishing boats, too. Germany is famous for the things it makes. Cars, ships, clothes, and clocks are all things that are made in Germany.

Gregor Schmid/Corbis

Owen Franken/Corbis

Gregor Schmid/Corbis

Dresden •

• Worms

Oberammergau •   *Chiemsee*

Man And
Woman
Fish With
Nets On
Chiemsee

Open Air Cafe In Regensburg

Hamburg

Wiesbaden

Regensburg

Baden-Baden

Adam Woolfitt/Corbis

Food

Germans love to eat and cook. Dishes with vegetables and meats are especially popular. *Sauerkraut* (SOW–er-krowt) is a favorite dish made from cabbage. A chunky potato salad called *kartoffelsalat* (kar–TOF–fel-sa-lat) is also delicious. For dessert, many Germans make sweet **strudels**, or pastries. Strudels often have fruit fillings and creamy icing on top.

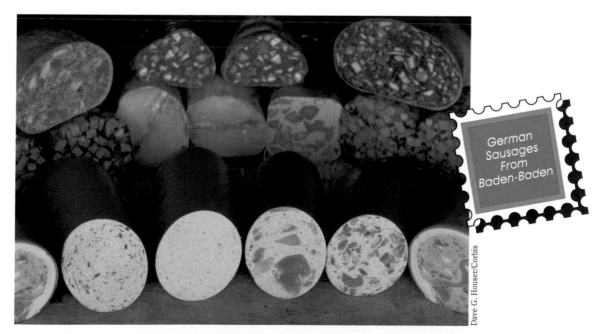

Pastimes

People in Germany love the outdoors. Hiking, bicycling, skiing, swimming, and sailing are all popular pastimes in Germany. Some people also like to go rock climbing up the country's steep mountains. Talking with friends and spending time with family members are important pastimes, too.

Soccer is the most popular sport in Germany. People play it in parks, in fields, on streets, and in yards. There are also professional soccer teams that play in huge stadiums across the country. Other popular sports in Germany are tennis, volleyball, and basketball.

Skiing Down To Kreuzeck Mountain Restaurant

Adam Woolfitt/Corbis

The Zugspitze, Germany's Highest Peak, Is Easy To Reach

Ric Ergenbright/Corbis

Adam Woolfitt/Corbis

Windsurfing And Sailing On Hopfensee

BAVARIA

Hopfensee

Kreuzeck Mountain + + Zugspitze

Adam Woolfitt/Corbis

Crowds Fill The Halls At Munich's Oktoberfest

FORMER WEST GERMANY

FORMER EAST GERMANY

Berlin

Idstein

BAVARIA
Munich

Bob Krist/Corbis

Holidays

Fairground Rides At Oktoberfest

Adam Woolfitt/Corbis

Germans love parties and festivals. They celebrate everything from birthdays and holidays to good harvests. One special German celebration is German Unity Day. On this day, people remember when East and West Germany were reunited after World War II.

Another fun German celebration is called **Oktoberfest**. For 16 days in the fall, Germans enjoy lots of food. They laugh and sing as bands play happy tunes. Oktoberfest isn't really celebrating anything. It is a festival that started almost 200 years ago at a prince's wedding.

José F. Poblete/Corbis

Medieval Fair In Idstein

Many people think that Germany is one of the nicest countries in the world. If you get the chance to visit Germany, look around. Talk to some people and eat some German food. Maybe you'll think Germany is great, too!

New Year's Fun On The Berlin Wall After Unity

Owen Franken/Corbis

29

Saint Coloman Church In Bavaria

Did You
Know?

Germany is really called the "Federal Republic of Germany."
People just say "Germany" for short.

Germans love to make different sausages from all kinds of
meat. Bratwurst and frankfurters are two sausages that come
from German recipes.

Many famous music writers, or **composers**, have come from
Germany. Johann Sebastian Bach and Ludwig van
Beethoven are two composers who created beautiful music.

Germany once had a king named Ludwig II. He liked to build
castles that were very expensive. One castle, called
Neuschwanstein (noy–SHVAN–stine) was very big and
beautiful. Walt Disney used it as a model for the castle in the
movie Sleeping Beauty. There is a picture of Neuschwanstein
castle on page 2 of this book.

How
Do You
Say?

	GERMAN	HOW TO SAY IT
Hello	guten tag	(GOOT–nn TAHK)
Goodbye	auf wiedersehen	(AWF VEE–der–zay–hen)
Please	bitte	(BIH–teh)
Thank You	danke	(DAHN–keh)
One	eins	(EYE-nnts)
Two	zwei	(TSVY)
Three	drei	(DRY)
Germany	Deutschland	(DOYTCH–lant)

Glossary

composers (kom–POH–zerz)
Composers are people who write music. Many famous composers came from Germany.

continents (KON–tih–nents)
Most of the land areas on Earth are divided up into huge sections called continents. Germany is on the continent of Europe.

immigrants (IM–mih–grents)
An immigrant is a newcomer from another country. Some Germans are immigrants.

Oktoberfest (ok–TOH–ber–fest)
Oktoberfest is a German festival that lasts for 16 days. During Oktoberfest, people eat, drink, sing, and listen to music.

strudels (STROO–delz)
Strudels are sweet German pastries. Many strudels have fruit fillings and thick icing.

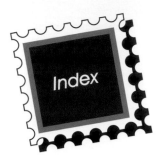

Index

Alps, 8, 9, 18

animals, 10, 18

Black Forest, 9

castles, 31

cities, 4, 18, 22

composers, 31

continents, 6

country life, 18

foods, 25, 29

German Unity Day, 4, 29

history, 13, 21

holidays, 4, 29

kartoffelsalat, 25

languages, 4, 21

lowlands, 9

Oktoberfest, 9, 28, 29

people, 4, 13, 14, 17, 18, 21, 22, 26, 29, 31

plants, 10

sauerkraut, 25

sausages, 25, 31

school, 21

soccer, 26

sports, 26

strudels, 25

work, 14, 22

World War I, 13

World War II, 14, 29